Football's All-Time Greats

RECEIVERS

JOSH LEVENTHAL

**BLACK
RABBIT
BOOKS**

Bolt is published by Black Rabbit Books
P.O. Box 3263, Mankato, Minnesota, 56002.
www.blackrabbitbooks.com
Copyright © 2017 Black Rabbit Books

Design and Production by Michael Sellner
Photo Research by Rhonda Milbrett

Library of Congress Control Number: 2015954849

HC ISBN: 978-1-68072-042-6   PB ISBN: 978-1-68072-300-7

Printed in the United States at CG Book Printers,
North Mankato, Minnesota, 56003. PO #1796 4/16

Web addresses included in this book were working and appropriate
at the time of publication. The publisher is not responsible for broken
or changed links.

Image Credits

Contents

CHAPTER 1

A Leaping Catch

The quarterback yells, "hike!" The receiver sprints down the field. He looks back. The ball is spiraling toward him. He leaps into the air and catches the ball. Touchdown!

RECEIVER'S CATCH

spread hands wide, keeping thumbs together

focus eyes on the ball

Step 1

Step 2

6

**look
through**
the hands

**catch the ball
with fingers**

**bring ball close
to the body**

Step 3

CHAPTER 2

Receivers

from 1920 to 1965

Receivers are an important part of a team's **offense**. Their main job is to catch passes. Receivers need to be fast runners. They also need strong hands. They must be quick thinkers too.

Long ago, receivers played both offense and **defense**. In the 1930s, teams started passing more. Receivers quickly became very important.

Don Hutson

Players in the Hall of Fame by Position
(through 2016)

Quarterbacks	Running Backs	Receivers	Tight Ends	Kickers/Punters	Linebackers
33	46	25	8	4	27

Don Hutson and Elroy Hirsch

Don Hutson was the first great receiver in the **NFL**. He played for the Packers. Hutson led the league in touchdowns nine times.

Elroy Hirsch was another great receiver. In 1951, he set a record with 1,495 **yards** gained on catches. His nickname was "Crazylegs." People said his legs looked like they moved in six directions when he ran.

Raymond Berry

Raymond Berry played 13 seasons for the Colts. He could find many ways to get open on the field. Berry only **fumbled** twice in his pro **career**.

Lance Alworth

Lance Alworth played in seven All-Star Games in the 1960s. He played for the Chargers. Alworth once caught passes in 96 straight games. That streak was a record at the time.

SIZE THEM UP

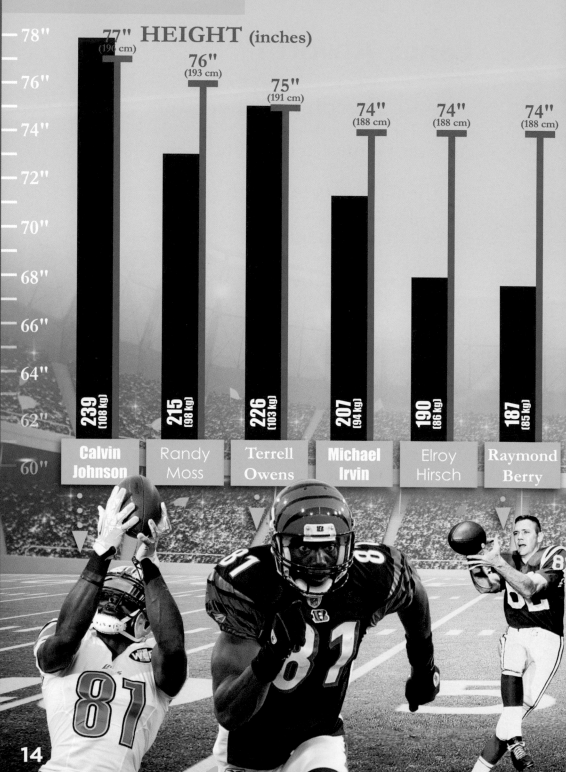

HEIGHT (inches)

78"
77" (196 cm)
76" (193 cm)
76"
75" (191 cm)
74" (188 cm)
74" (188 cm)
74" (188 cm)
74"
72"
70"
68"
66"
64"
62"
60"

239 (108 kg) — Calvin Johnson
215 (98 kg) — Randy Moss
226 (103 kg) — Terrell Owens
207 (94 kg) — Michael Irvin
190 (86 kg) — Elroy Hirsch
187 (85 kg) — Raymond Berry

WEIGHT
(pounds)

240
235
230
225
220
215
210
205
200
195
190
185
180
175
170
165
160
155
150

74"
(188 cm)

73"
(185 cm)

72"
(183 cm)

72"
(183 cm)

71"
(180cm)

69"
(175 cm)

190
(86 kg)

183
(83 kg)

184
(83 kg)

175
(79 kg)

187
(85 kg)

190
(86 kg)

Jerry
Rice

Don
Hutson

Lance
Alworth

Marvin
Harrison

Steve
Largent

Wes
Welker

15

CHAPTER 3

Receivers

from 1966 to 1999

Passing became even more popular in the 1970s. Rule changes limited where **defenders** could hit receivers. These new rules made it easier for receivers to get open.

Steve Largent

Rice's
Career
Records

most catches	most receiving yards
1,549	**22,895**

Jerry Rice and Steve Largent

Many people think Jerry Rice is the greatest receiver of all time. He caught more passes than anybody in history. He scored more touchdowns too. Rice played mostly for the 49ers.

Steve Largent played 14 years with the Seahawks. When he **retired**, his 819 catches were a record. His 100 touchdown catches were also a record at the time.

most touchdowns	most seasons with 50 or more catches	most seasons with 1,000 or more receiving yards
207	**17**	**14**

Michael Irvin and Marvin Harrison

Michael Irvin played for the Cowboys. He was nicknamed "the playmaker" for his exciting catches. He made 750 catches in 159 games.

Marvin Harrison played with the Colts for 13 seasons. He and quarterback Peyton Manning were a fantastic team. Together, they connected for 112 touchdowns.

Most Catches
in One Season

143	136	136	129	123	123
Marvin Harrison	Antonio Brown	Julio Jones	Antonio Brown	Herman Moore	Wes Welker

(through 2015)

CHAPTER 4

Receivers
from 2000 to Today

Today, passing is more popular than ever. New rules protect quarterbacks and receivers even more. These rules give teams more freedom to pass.

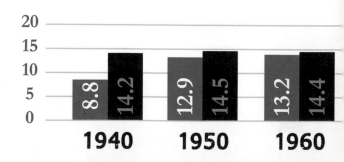

Terrell Owens

Average Catches Per Game vs. Yards Per Catch

| 13.8 | 13.2 | 17.3 | 12.9 | 16.9 | 12.5 | 19.1 | 11.6 | 20.5 | 11.5 |
| 1970 | | 1980 | | 1990 | | 2000 | | 2010 | |

Randy Moss

Terrell Owens and Randy Moss

Terrell Owens was a star receiver for 15 years. He holds the third-place record for receiving touchdowns. He caught 153 touchdowns in his career.

Randy Moss was sometimes called "the freak." He had great speed and could leap high. Defenders had a hard time stopping him. His 23 touchdowns in 2007 are a record for one season.

Wes Welker

Wes Welker played
for the Dolphins,
Patriots, and Broncos.
Now he plays with
the Rams. With the
Patriots, Welker caught
more than 110 passes
in five different
seasons. Nobody
else has done that.

Calvin Johnson

Calvin Johnson holds the record for most receiving yards in one season. He had 1,964 yards with the Lions in 2012.

Catching for the Win

Receivers catch more passes than ever before. They are also faster and stronger. Teams need these amazing athletes. Their catches can lead them to the win.

1925

October 1929
Great Depression begins

September 1939
World War II begins

1942
Don Hutson
earns 1,000 receiving yards
in a season.

July 1969
first moon landing

1961
Lionel Taylor
catches 100 passes
in one season.

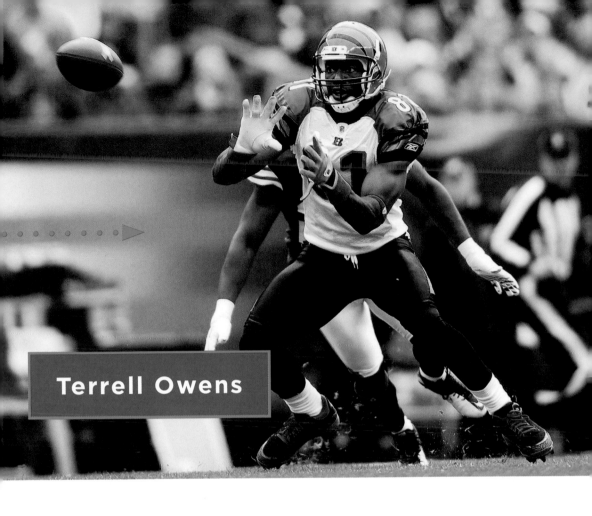

Terrell Owens

September 2001
terrorist attack on World
Trade Center and Pentagon

2000
Terrell Owens catches
20 passes in one game.

2007
Randy Moss
has 23 touchdowns
in one season.

2015

GLOSSARY

career (kuh-REER)—a period of time spent in a job

defender (de-FEN-dur)—a player who is assigned to a defensive position

defense (DEE-fens)—the players on a team who try to stop the other team from scoring

fumble (FUM-buhl)—a ball that is loose because a player failed to hold on to it

NFL—short for National Football League

offense (AW-fens)—the group of players in control of the ball trying to score points

retire (ree-TIYR)—to stop playing a game or competition

yard (YARD)—a unit of length; one yard equals 3 feet (1 meter).

BOOKS

Bodden, Valerie. *Calvin Johnson.* The Big Time. Mankato, MN: Creative Education, 2015.

Challen, Paul. *What Does a Receiver Do?* Football Smarts. New York: PowerKids Press, 2015.

Scheff, Matt. *Superstars of the Dallas Cowboys.* Pro Sports Superstars. Mankato, MN: Amicus, 2014.

WEBSITES

Football: Receivers
www.ducksters.com/sports/football/wide_receiver.php

Football's Offensive Team: The Receivers
www.dummies.com/how-to/content/footballs-offensive-team-the-receivers.html

Pro Football Hall of Fame
www.profootballhof.com

INDEX